HOLIDAY
HACKS

**Easy Solutions to Simplify
the Most ~~Wonderful~~ STRESSFUL
Time of the Year**

Keith Bradford

Adams Media

New York   London   Toronto   Sydney   New Delhi

Adams Media
An Imprint of Simon & Schuster, Inc.
57 Littlefield Street
Avon, Massachusetts 02322

First Adams Media trade paperback edition October 2018

For information about special discounts for bulk purchases, please contact Simon & Schuster Special Sales at 1-866-506-1949 or business@simonandschuster.com.

The Simon & Schuster Speakers Bureau can bring authors to your live event. For more information or to book an event contact the Simon & Schuster Speakers Bureau at 1-866-248-3049 or visit our website at www.simonspeakers.com.

Interior design by Katrina Machado
Interior images © Getty Images/AndyMcFly, redchocolatte, ExpressIPhoto, Mochipet, Nikiteev_Konstantin, Baksiabat, girafchik123, FrankRamspott, Shiffarigum, lemonadeserenade, BlackStork, yhloon, AllAGRI

Manufactured in the United States of America

10 9 8 7 6 5 4 3 2

Library of Congress Cataloging-in-Publication Data
Bradford, Keith, 1989- author.
Holiday hacks / Keith Bradford.
Avon, Massachusetts: Adams Media, 2018.
Series: Hacks.
LCCN 2018016829 (print) | LCCN 2018017647 (ebook) | ISBN 9781507208571 (pb) | ISBN 9781507208588 (ebook)
Subjects: LCSH: Holiday decorations. | Holiday cooking. | Entertaining. | BISAC: REFERENCE / Personal & Practical Guides. | REFERENCE / Trivia. | HOUSE & HOME / General.
Classification: LCC TT900.H6 (ebook) | LCC TT900.H6 B73 2018 (print) | DDC 745.594/16--dc23
LC record available at https://lccn.loc.gov/2018016829

ISBN 978-1-5072-0857-1
ISBN 978-1-5072-0858-8 (ebook)

Contents

Introduction

It's the most wonderful time of the year! And the most hectic, expensive, and stressful time of the year too! A season filled with long shopping lists, tangled lights, over-sugared children, bickering relatives, crowded malls, and sky-high expectations. Well, not to worry—*Holiday Hacks* is here to help.

Between these pages we've collected more than six hundred hacks to help you get your holiday in line and simplify all of the tasks that come between you and a peaceful celebration, so you can enjoy your holiday to the fullest. We've gathered secret tips and shortcuts to prepare for the holiday, decorate your house, cook your holiday dinner, host a gathering for family and friends, and then pack it all up and hit the New Year running.

The hacks in this book are broken down into chapters centered on certain themes—like food and drinks, shopping, and the holiday aftermath—to help lead you through the season, so you can read the section where you need the most help or just flip to any page for a quick fix. Whatever you need help with, we've got you covered, so turn to any page and start improving your holidays (and your sanity!) right now!

Chapter 1
Deck the Halls

1. Trying to put holiday lights up on bricks? Use a hot glue gun to fasten them on. The glue won't damage the brick, and you can rip the lights off in seconds at the end of the season.

2. Your festive holiday candles will burn longer and drip less on your tablecloth if they are placed in the freezer a few hours before you use them.

3. Use some binder clips to help secure your outdoor lights to the roof.

4. Make the perfect place card holders for your guests out of candy canes! Put glue down the stick side of one candy cane and attach a second cane to it, stick to stick, so the "hooks" face away from each other. Add more glue and attach a third cane in the back for stability. Turn the canes upside down so the hook sections are on the table, and lay the place card in the curve of the hooks.

5. Don't have the time to decorate the outside of your house this year? Try using a laser projector. You can create your own festive designs, and the projector covers the entire house.

6. When shoveling snow to make room for all your decorations, spray your shovel with nonstick cooking spray before you go out. The snow will slide off easily, making shoveling a breeze.

7. Draw some snowflakes or festive designs on your windows using a hot glue gun. It's super easy to draw with, and the glue is even easier to remove.

8. Get a perfect-looking front porch by using a broom to clear the snow rather than a shovel.

Ten Ways to Keep Your House Warm This Holiday Without Running Up Your Heating Bill

9. Leave your oven door open after you cook.
10. Open the curtains when the sun is out.
11. Use quilts instead of curtains—the thicker, the better.
12. Light some candles. Not only do they set a festive mood, but they'll also warm up the surrounding area.
13. Cut open a tube of pipe insulation or a pool noodle vertically, and attach the pieces to the bottom of your doors. This will help seal in heat and keep the frosty air out.
14. Put your ceiling fan on low and run it counter-clockwise (in reverse). Hot air rises, so this will help evenly distribute the heat.

15. Insulate yourself with a layer of running tights or pantyhose.
16. Close the doors to rooms you're not using. This will help keep the heat in one area.
17. Put a layer of tinfoil on the wall across from your wall-mounted radiator or heater. The heat will bounce back and fill the room better.
18. Place some rugs, carpeting, or old quilts over your floor.

19. Wrapping paper getting crinkly and messy? Grab an old wine crate from your local wine store for a simple wrapping paper holder. The deep compartments that used to hold the wine bottles will hold your paper perfectly.

20. Easily run lights down your railings by attaching them with zip ties.

21. The best Christmas fire starter: grab all that built-up lint from your dryer, stuff it into an old toilet paper roll, and wrap it in wax paper.

22. Fill your shoe trays with some pebbles before putting guests' wet boots or shoes on them. This allows the water to drain away easily and gives the boots a quicker drying period.

23. Don't burn yourself trying to light those hard-to-reach, burned-down candles. Light a piece of raw spaghetti and use it to light the wicks.

24. Trying to hang up a decoration but the screw is stripped? Place a rubber band over the screwdriver head and try again. The rubber will fill in the gaps, making it easy to screw in or out.

25. Make your house smell amazing and festive this season by boiling some orange peels with ½ teaspoon of cinnamon and about 4–5 cups of water over medium heat.

26. Have some leftover gingerbread cookies? You can turn them into ornaments by adding a layer of varnish over them. They'll be good for years.

27. The easiest way to start a cozy holiday fire: use cotton balls slathered in petroleum jelly. Put a few under the firewood, and light them up for an easy and instant fire starter.

28. Place your scented candles near the door of your room or house. They will be the first thing guests smell on entry, even if they are unlit.

29. Have some old pumpkins lying around from Halloween? Spray-paint them white, and stack three on top of each other for a unique DIY snowman.

30. No need to put a nail in your door to hang a wreath. Place an upside-down Command hook on the inside of your door, tie a ribbon around the top of your wreath, run the ribbon over the top of your door, and then loop the ribbon over the hook and close the door.

31. No fireplace to snuggle up in front of this Christmas? On FreeFireplaces.com you can get a full-screen loop of a digital fireplace.

32. Icy doorsteps but no salt? Pour a bucket of warm water with dishwashing soap on them. The soap won't let the water refreeze.

33. Have a broken umbrella lying around? Spray-paint it white, string some lights on it, and hang it upside down. It's like a festive DIY chandelier.

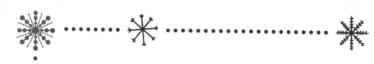

34. Want to avoid snowplows dumping a load of snow in front of your driveway and ruining the look of your perfect holiday décor? Clear the snowy area to the left of your driveway, and the plow will have nothing to push in front of your driveway.

35. Christmas tree lights too bright? Dull them by putting Ping-Pong balls over them. It also gives your lights a whole new festive feel.

36. Hang ornaments from your chandelier for a unique, festive look.

37. If you're going to have guests under five years old for the holidays, hang your decorations as high as possible.

38. One of the best ways to start your holiday fire is with orange peels. They burn well due to the oils found on their skins, plus they make your fire smell great!

39. Using pinecones as decorations? Bake them first for forty-five minutes at 200°F to make sure you get all the bugs/larvae out of the nooks and crannies.

Ten DIY Christmas Tree Alternatives

40. Use a big chalkboard and draw your own tree.
41. Make a tree-shaped photo collage of your past year's memories.
42. String lights on your wall in the shape of a tree.
43. Pin branches from fallen trees to your wall.
44. Decorate a Christmas cactus.
45. Get a photo of a Christmas tree blown up as a poster.
46. Tape Christmas cards from past years in rows to form a triangle.
47. Cut out your own tree from Christmas wrapping paper, and use double-sided tape to stick it to the wall.
48. Label twenty-five sticky notes, and put one up on the wall each day in December until you form a Christmas tree.
49. A tree-shaped stack of your favorite books makes for a unique tree alternative.

50. Place all your wrapping paper in a garment bag for easy, portable, and clutter-free storage.

51. Too lazy to decorate? Just throw a Santa hat on your leftover Halloween pumpkin.

52. Want to have a fire in your fireplace but dread having to clean it up? Try a tinfoil fire cleaner: place two layers of tinfoil down as a base before you start your fire. After the fire dies, grab the two ends for easy cleanup.

53. Make your home smell festive by adding cinnamon and essential oils to a pot with 4–5 cups water and boiling it over medium heat. Your house will smell like Christmas in no time, and this mix will also help humidify the air.

54. Taking some Christmas photos? Try having guests laugh for the camera. It always looks more natural than holding a fake smile.

55. Speaking of Christmas photos: keep in mind that on camera, wearing yellow makes you look bigger, and wearing green makes you look smaller.

56. Christmas ornaments don't just belong on your tree. Try hanging them on chandeliers, banisters, open doors, mantels, and so on for a unique, festive feel throughout your home.

57. Bring your house to life by outlining your doorways with some leftover garland or lights from your Christmas tree.

58. Make a unique Christmas card hanger by stringing lights on the inside of a large, empty picture frame. Hang your cards from the light strings, and you have a Christmas work of art.

59. Want your home to feel warmer during the winter months? Paint your walls red, orange, or yellow. These colors have been proven to evoke feelings of happiness, optimism, and warmth.

60. Make decorating stress-free by picking a color palette in advance. Say, for example, that you choose red as your focal color; now your decorating choices are easier, and your entire house will be color-coordinated!

61. Spruce up your picture frames around the house by filling them with some leftover wrapping paper.

62. A fun way to get into the spirit of the season is to make a feel-good Advent calendar: randomly fill twenty-four envelopes with slips of paper that have good deeds written on them. Open one envelope each day starting on December 1, and perform that deed within twenty-four hours.

63. Wrap your Christmas cookie cutters in ribbon for simple DIY ornaments.

64. Save money on a wreath by making your own out of your tree trimmings. Fan the branches out into a star, tie them together, and add some red sprigs of fake berries from a dollar store.

65. Christmas wreath looking a little bare? You can add a layer to it by sticking some leaves from your lawn into the sides.

Chapter 2
Food and Drink

66. What says the holidays better than a cup of steaming hot chocolate? And the best (and easiest) way to make a hot chocolate is to put a scoop of Nutella in warm milk and stir.

67. Want your holiday meal to have the fluffiest mashed potatoes ever? Add a pinch of baking powder while mashing. The heat from the potatoes will mix with the baking powder and make tiny air pockets.

68. You can make stale Christmas cookies soft again by putting them in a plastic bag with a piece of bread. Leave the cookies in the bag overnight, and they'll be almost as good as new.

69. Crush up candy canes into a fine powder. Then save the powder to sprinkle into your hot chocolate, cake batter, cookies, ice cream, and so on for a festive touch.

70. Cooking your holiday meal when you get an overflow on the stove? If your water starts foaming over the edge of the pot when you're boiling it, pour in a couple tablespoons of olive oil. It'll stop overflowing almost instantly.

71. Don't have a roasting rack to cook your holiday turkey on? Make one yourself by crafting some tinfoil into a doughnut-like circle and placing your turkey on top.

72. Spice up your cup of cheer by making your whipped cream unique. Spread the whipped cream on a cookie sheet, freeze it, and then cut it into shapes with different cookie cutters.

73. Make Christmas breakfast easy: put pancake batter in a clean ketchup bottle to make a ton of pancakes fast! You can even use this hack to make fun holiday shapes.

74. Make sure to stock up on butter at the start of the holiday season. Almost every recipe uses it, and you'll never have to run out to the store at an awkward time.

Ten Ways to Spice Up Your Holiday Hot Chocolate

75. **Peppermint:** 1 cup whole milk, ½ cup chocolate chips, 1 teaspoon peppermint extract.

76. **Orange:** 1 cup milk, ½ tablespoon sugar, ½ tablespoon grated orange zest, 2 ounces dark chocolate.

77. **Vegan:** 1 cup vanilla almond milk, 1½ tablespoons unsweetened cocoa powder, 2 teaspoons coconut palm sugar.

78. **Aztec:** 1 cup milk, 5 ounces chopped dark chocolate, ¼ teaspoon cinnamon, a pinch of cayenne.

79. **Peanut Butter:** 1 cup skim milk, ½ cup heavy cream, 4 ounces chopped milk chocolate, ¼ cup creamy peanut butter.

80. **Pumpkin Spice:** 1 cup whole milk, 1 teaspoon maple syrup, ½ teaspoon pumpkin pie spice, 1 teaspoon unsweetened dark cocoa.

81. **Nutella:** 1 cup whole milk, 2 tablespoons Nutella, 1 tablespoon cocoa, a pinch of salt.
82. **Caramel:** ½ cup milk, 5 ounces chopped milk chocolate, ¼ cup heavy cream, 3 tablespoons caramel sauce.
83. **Lavender White:** 1 cup whole milk, ¼ teaspoon lavender buds, ½ cup white chocolate chips.
84. **Irish:** 1 cup milk, ½ cup chocolate chips, 2 ounces Baileys Irish Cream.

85. When you want to put a 2-liter bottle of soda away, shake it up a little bit first. It will stay fizzy for weeks.

86. Taking warm food to a Christmas party? Put it on your passenger seat and turn on the seat warmer.

87. An old Pringles can makes a perfect cookie gift box. Simply wrap the outside with some festive wrapping paper and stack the cookies inside.

88. Mash your holiday potatoes using warm milk only. Cold milk will make your potatoes turn gray.

89. Want to keep your skin moist and supple during the harsh winter months? You can do it with food! Add some fish oil, olive oil, nuts, flaxseeds, and avocados to your diet.

90. Keep your gravy warm throughout the entire Christmas dinner by storing it in a thermos.

91. Want to keep all your fingers intact this holiday? Lay a kitchen towel underneath your cutting board to keep it from slipping.

92. Reheating leftover stuffing? Microwave it with a small amount of water in a glass. This will make sure it doesn't get hard or chewy.

93. Not enough stove space to cook your Christmas dinner? You can store things like mashed potatoes, soups, squash, and so on in a slow cooker over low heat.

94. Making Christmas cookies and don't have eggs? Sure, you could ask the neighbor, but half of a banana (per egg) works as a great substitute.

95. Keep your ice cream ready for scooping onto your holiday treats by storing your ice cream tubs inside zip-top freezer bags in your freezer. This will keep the ice cream soft and ready for use.

96. Save your old aluminum foil and plastic wrap containers. Simply wrap them in festive paper or decorate them, and then they make perfect little boxes for gifting cookies.

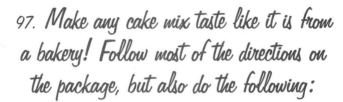

97. Make any cake mix taste like it is from a bakery! Follow most of the directions on the package, but also do the following:

> * Add one more egg (or two for an even richer taste).
> * Replace oil with melted butter and double the amount.
> * Replace water with an equal amount of milk.

Then mix and bake the cake according to the package. Your holiday guests need never know it was a boxed cake mix!

98. Need to cook multiple dishes in your oven for your holiday dinner? You can expand it with a tiered oven rack—perfect for cooking multiple pies or casseroles.

99. Want a quick and easy holiday dessert topping? Crush up Oreo cookies and put them in a salt grinder. Now you can instantly add chocolate goodness to your desserts without all the mess.

100. Make a chalkboard serving platter to label food for your guests. Here's what to do:

* Paint a serving dish with black chalkboard paint.
* Let it dry overnight.
* Label your snacks with a piece of standard chalk.

101. Ready to carve your holiday turkey when you realize you have only dull knives? In a pinch you can sharpen a knife by cutting through some pieces of aluminum foil.

102. Carving knives dull and no aluminum foil left? Flip a ceramic mug over and scrape the blade against the rough edge. The knife will cut almost like it's brand-new!

103. Use condiment bottles filled with icing for an easy way to decorate Christmas cookies and cakes.

104. Having trouble cooking your Christmas dinner? Call Butterball's Turkey Talk-Line at 1-800-BUTTERBALL (1-800-288-8372). They'll help you with any Christmas cooking problems free of charge.

105. Don't want to wear remnants of your holiday dinner all over your fancy clothes? Sprinkling a little salt in your frying pan will prevent any oil from splattering all over you and your stove.

106. Need to buy ice cream for your holiday desserts? In the store, press on the top of the ice cream container. If it feels solid, it's been properly stored. If it can be pushed down, it's been thawed and refrozen.

107. Need to make a big batch of hot chocolate? Make it in a slow cooker.

108. Make some Creamy Christmas Cocoa:

1½ cups heavy cream,
1 (14-ounce) can sweetened condensed
milk, 2 cups milk chocolate chips,
6 cups milk, and 1 teaspoon vanilla
extract. Mix, heat, and serve!

109. Never put Christmas dinner leftovers in the fridge when they are still warm. The container covers act as insulators and the meat inside will stay warm longer, which attracts bacteria and allows it to thrive!

110. Butter too hard to cut or spread? Use a cheese grater.

111. Try cooking your stuffing in a muffin tin this year. The clumps stick together, making them easier to serve and more fun to eat!

112. Before buying a turkey, measure your oven. Larger birds might not fit in some ovens, and there's nothing worse than finding *that* out on Christmas morning.

113. A few drops of green food coloring and some M&M's will turn your Rice Krispies Treats into a festive snack.

114. Need to save some space in your fridge for all that holiday food? Cut off the unused sections of your egg cartons.

115. Making fudge this year? Make it with holiday-themed cookie cutters for a more festive touch.

116. Is your gravy lacking that certain something? Try adding a dash of soy sauce. It's high in sodium, so it can really bring your gravy back to life.

117. When heating leftover turkey, space out a circle in the middle of the food. The empty space will help your food heat up much more evenly.

118. Make the freshest Christmas dinner: grocery stores stack their products by sell-by date, which means the oldest food is in the front. Make sure to always grab food from the back.

119. Did you overcook the turkey a little bit? Pour some chicken broth over the entire thing. This will give it the much-needed moisture it needs without taking away the flavor.

120. To make fluffier white rice, add a teaspoon of lemon juice to the boiling water before you put the rice in the pot.

121. Try baking your Christmas cookies in a muffin tin. They'll stay soft and fluffy, and they won't spread out as thin as they normally would.

122. When buying your food for your holiday meals, keep in mind that in most grocery stores, the cheapest items will be on the top and bottom shelves, not at eye level.

123. Keep an eye on food items in the days after Thanksgiving. There are a lot of sales on things that can be served at Christmas too.

124. Take a picture of your fridge and pantry with your phone before you go grocery shopping. You'll never forget anything at the store again!

125. Never go shopping at the grocery store when you are hungry. You'll end up buying several things you don't actually need.

Chapter 3

Shopping, Shipping, and Wrapping

126. Mailing out some Christmas cards? On MailboxLocate.com you can enter your location and get directions to the closest mailbox.

127. Sending out a lot of holiday cards this year? Try sending postcards instead. Postage is thirty-five cents versus fifty cents for a card. Plus, you'll save on not having to buy envelopes too.

128. Save yourself from having to wrap gifts until the wee hours of Christmas morning by wrapping them as you buy them.

129. Want to save even more on holiday cards? Send e-cards instead.

130. When you are Christmas shopping, pay for things in cash. Studies have shown you're more likely to be conservative with cash than with a credit card.

131. Usually have trouble thinking of what you want for Christmas? Write a Christmas list all year round. This also works great for thinking of gifts to get for people.

132. Getting a new puppy or kitten for Christmas? Don't feed it first thing in the morning. This way it will grow up having no reason to wake you up in the morning.

133. Many stores will price match an item if you bring in proof of the reduced price. Keep an eye on prices this holiday season, and you may save yourself some dough.

134. Forget to put something in that holiday package? Placing an envelope in the fridge for an hour will help unseal it.

135. Forget clipping out coupons by hand. RetailMeNot.com is like a digital coupon book—all you have to do is show your phone at checkout.

136. Have some old paint swatches lying around? Cut them into tree, stocking, or gingerbread man shapes, and you'll have some unique and attractive gift tags.

137. Don't know what to get people for Christmas? Have them make three guesses of what you bought them. You now have three ideas for what to get them!

138. Can't find someone to help you in an electronics store? Stand by the biggest, most expensive TV and look at the price tag. Someone will be right over.

139. Looking for a camera to document all your holiday festivities? Go to Flickr.com/Cameras; you can browse photos by the camera they were shot on.

140. Having gifts shipped to you? Don't bother going to those confusing shipping websites! Simply type your package number into *Google*, and it'll take you straight to the tracking page.

141. Finding it hard to know what to write in your Christmas cards? Take a look at other cards in the card store for some great ideas that you can borrow.

142. Always ask for a discount when buying jewelry. You'll usually be able to get a good one.

143. Want a more professional-looking wrapping job? Use double-sided tape on the inside of the wrapping paper.

144. Don't use a shopping basket at a store unless you really have to. It's been proven that carrying a shopping bag or basket makes the average consumer buy more.

145. When signing up on retail websites, say that your birthday is December 1. That way you'll get promotional birthday vouchers that you can use to save money on Christmas gifts.

146. The ShopSavvy app lets you scan bar codes when you're shopping and tells you if you can get the item elsewhere for cheaper.

147. Having trouble getting those annoying bar-code or price-tag stickers off your gifts? Rub a cloth soaked in vinegar over them to instantly remove the stickers and the goo they leave behind.

148. Cut open a toilet paper roll and use it as a cuff to save your wrapping paper from unrolling.

149. If you find an item somewhere else for cheaper, ask the store manager to match the price. You'd be surprised how many times managers will do it, even if it's not a store's policy.

150. *Tired of searching for your car in those never-ending mall parking lots? Take a picture as soon as you park there. Try to include the floor and row number painted on a pillar or wall for an easy find.*

151. Make transporting your gifts easier and give any Christmas gift its own handle by attaching some rope to the top.

152. Do you have any special skills? Give people the gift of your services, like a free photography session or a portrait of their pet.

153. Gift buying tip: never buy anyone a pet as a present unless you have previously arranged it.

154. Make your Christmas shopping easier by keeping a gift list on your phone throughout the year. Update it whenever you see or hear a good gift idea for someone.

155. Rather than buying physical things, buy people experiences like parachute jumps, paintball vouchers, guitar lessons, concert tickets, and so on. Other gifts can get forgotten and eventually turn into clutter. Experiences last a lifetime.

156. This year when your friends ask you what you want for Christmas, just say "Your favorite book." You'll get a mini library of awesome reading material that your friends built!

157. Catch up on your social media fix, texts, or emails while you're standing in the checkout line. Most stores have jewelry, cheap socks, and other impulse buys that you don't need. Do anything you can to distract yourself from these sections.

158. When buying something online, read only the reviews that give the item three stars. These reviews are usually the most honest about the pros and cons.

159. Make sure to install the Honey browser extension (JoinHoney.com) before doing your online holiday shopping. It adds coupon codes for discounts found around the Internet when you check out.

160. Planning on giving out gift cards this holiday season? You can buy them at up to 35 percent off their value from CardCash.com.

161. Worried you're using your credit card too much this holiday season? You can set up an automated text message that alerts you whenever you use your credit card. Almost all companies offer this service, and it also provides additional security.

162. Want to save some cash during the holidays? Send candy boxes that weigh less than 13 ounces. You don't have to repackage it; just slap on a stamp and address, and then toss it in the mail.

Ten Crafty Alternatives to Wrapping Paper

163. Map pages from an old atlas

164. Brown paper grocery bags

165. Pages from your local newspaper

166. Sheet music

167. Scrap pieces of fabric

168. An inside-out chip bag

169. Last season's ugly Christmas sweater

170. Pages from a word search or puzzle book

171. A festive scarf

172. Cereal boxes

173. To save money when you're Christmas shopping, don't touch anything. Touching an item makes you more likely to buy it and be willing to pay more for it.

174. On CheapRiver.com you can search for products on non-US versions of *Amazon* to find the cheapest possible price.

175. Try placing a paper clip on the end of your tape so that you never lose your place in the tape roll when wrapping presents.

176. If you want to buy a new laptop, phone, or other electronic device for Christmas, get it in October. You can usually get up to 40 percent off most electronics.

177. When shopping online, search for promo codes on *Google* before making a purchase. You can usually find a variety of discounts from free shipping to 25 percent off.

178. Save money on gifts by buying items that are in the off-season, like outdoor grills, swimwear, gardening equipment, golf clubs, and so on.

179. If you are shipping a fragile gift this holiday, the best way to pack the box is to pack it as if people will be trying to break it.

180. Forget something on Christmas Day? Most Asian-owned stores and restaurants are open.

181. Out shopping with the kids when they see something they want for Christmas? Snap a quick photo of it for easy reference later.

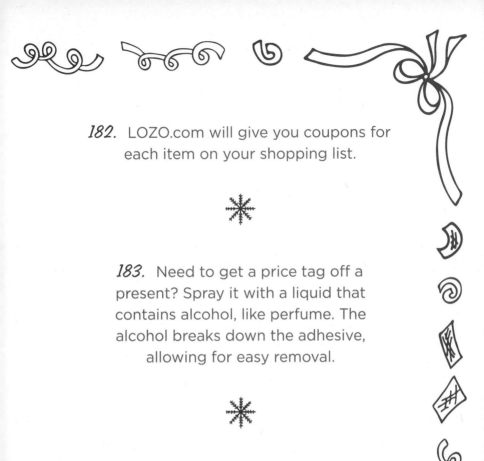

182. LOZO.com will give you coupons for each item on your shopping list.

❋

183. Need to get a price tag off a present? Spray it with a liquid that contains alcohol, like perfume. The alcohol breaks down the adhesive, allowing for easy removal.

❋

184. Newspaper makes for cool, unique wrapping paper. Every present looks different, it gives each present that rustic and vintage look that is so popular now, and you can usually get your hands on it for free.

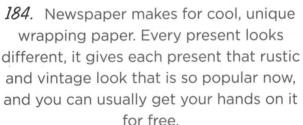

185. The Santa's Bag app helps you budget all your holiday shopping. It makes sure you don't forget anyone on your list and keeps you under your set budget so you don't go broke!

186. Broke holiday tip: the holidays are never a mandatory expense. If you're struggling financially this year, your friends and family will understand if you don't get them anything. Just make sure to tell them well in advance.

187. Buy one or two backup gifts and wrap them. There's nothing worse than forgetting to buy someone a gift.

Ten Gifts You Should Never Give Someone

188. **Pets:** Never get someone a living creature unless they have specifically asked for it.
189. **Regifted items:** Just in case they find out.
190. **DVDs:** Pretty soon they'll just be dust collectors.
191. **Exercise gear:** You don't want to insinuate the wrong thing.
192. **Airline tickets:** There's nothing worse than a trip you didn't get to plan.
193. **Cash:** Unless the person is under twenty, don't give cash. It's awkward.
194. **Romance novels:** Opening up *Fifty Shades of Grey* in front of your relatives might be a little embarrassing.
195. **Cleaning supplies:** Boring, and on top of that, it can come off as rude.
196. **Lingerie:** Privately to your wife, it's okay, but to anyone else, just no!
197. **Donations:** Don't give a donation in someone's name unless you 100 percent know they support the cause.

198. Always make a game plan before hitting the mall. Go to the mall's website beforehand; you can usually get a map and directory of the stores to plan your attack.

199. Try to find the hidden cashier at the store. There's usually some sort of courtesy counter or service desk in the store with an employee who can ring you out. These desks are often in unusual places like the back of the store, so keep an eye out.

Chapter 4

Christmas Tree, O Christmas Tree

200. When picking a Christmas tree, be aware that Fraser fir, noble fir, and Douglas fir trees will retain moisture better and therefore last the longest.

201. Use gardening gloves when putting up your tree lights. This will save your hands some wear and tear.

202. Want your house to smell like Christmas? Buy a Douglas fir tree. It gives off that festive Christmas tree smell.

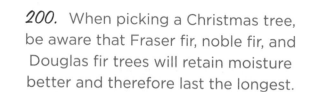

203. Try using bigger lights on the bottom of your tree and smaller lights on top. This gives the illusion that your tree is bigger than it actually is.

204. When setting up your Christmas tree, take a picture of the area beforehand so you can easily remember how everything looks when you have to put it all back.

205. Christmas tree looking a little bare? String some shiny green tinsel around the bare areas to make it look fuller.

Don't want a classic tree topper? Hack your own with one of these ten geeky tree topper alternatives:

206. A Death Star

207. Patrick Star the starfish

208. A King Kong action figure

209. A Super Mario Bros. star

210. A Darth Vader mask

211. A picture of your favorite movie star

212. Yoda

213. Godzilla

214. A Harry Potter Sorting Hat

215. A picture of Bill Murray

216. You can prolong the life of your tree by dropping a penny into the base and adding a pinch of sugar.

217. Did you get sticky tree sap all over your hands? Wash your hands with toothpaste, and it'll come right off.

218. Make sure to use a tree base that holds 1–1½ gallons of water. Trees can get thirsty and absorb up to 1 gallon per day!

219. String a line of lights down the center of your Christmas tree. You won't be able to see the lights, and it will give the illusion that it's glowing from within.

220. Tree decorating guide: for every 1 foot of tree height, you need one hundred lights, 9 feet of garland, and twenty ornaments.

221. Keep your kid's first pair of shoes. They make perfect Christmas tree ornaments.

222. Babyproof your tree by placing big, empty presents under it so your little one can't get to it.

223. If that doesn't work, you can always just put a playpen around the tree.

224. Don't fall for buying those fragile, shiny ornaments. You can get ones made from plastic, wood, straw, or cloth that won't break when they fall and will look just as good!

225. Cut off a slice of the bottom of your tree and turn it into a decoration. Simply take the slice and decorate it using a wood burner, permanent markers, or even Mod Podge glue with your favorite pictures. Then add a hook or hammer in a nail, and hang it on some festive ribbon.

226. Old tomato cages make perfect mini Christmas trees. Just turn one upside down and string some lights around it, and it will look fantastic! You can even hang a few ornaments off it.

227. Need some last-minute table décor? Clip a few branches off your tree.

228. *Always make sure you measure where you're planning to put your tree before going out to buy one.*

229. Want to use fewer lights on your Christmas tree? Place it in the corner, and string the lights in a zigzag pattern.

230. Make sure to pick up a disposable tree bag when you buy your tree. Most places sell these bags, and having one handy will make your life easier when cleanup time comes.

231. If you're buying a tree from a lot, make sure to saw off about an inch from the bottom when you get home. When trees are initially harvested, the cut oozes with pitch, sealing and clogging the transport cells that provide water to the needles.

Ten Christmas Tree Safety Tips

232. Buy fresh. The fresher and healthier the tree, the less likely it is to be a fire hazard.

233. Keep it hydrated. Making sure your tree stand always has water will make your tree less flammable.

234. Always have a fire extinguisher nearby, and make sure everyone in the house knows how to use it.

235. If you have an artificial tree with a metal base, don't use electric lights. The metal can act as a conductor and lead to electrocution.

236. Water your tree daily. The drier the branches, the more flammable your tree becomes.

237. Don't plug too many strings of lights into one extension cord.

238. Watch where you're stringing your lights to prevent any tripping hazards.

239. Never leave your lights on overnight. You can get a timed outlet to make sure this doesn't happen.

240. Use low-energy lights—they are proven to be safer, and will also help keep your electric bill low.

241. Never use any lights that look damaged or frayed, and certainly never try to fix old ones yourself.

242. Put a circular sled under the base of your tree to help catch any water spillage. If your tree is on a hardwood floor, place a mat under it for some extra grip.

243. The most expensive types of Christmas trees are balsam and Douglas firs, while the least expensive are Nordmann and Turkish firs.

244. Give boring glass ornaments a makeover with glitter and Pledge furniture polish. Pour some polish into the glass ball; swirl it around and pour out the excess; then add some glitter and swirl it around. Voilà! Glitter ornaments!

245. Experiment with your tree's lighting by overlapping another style or size of lights on top of the first set.

246. Decorating the trees outside your home? Cut a couple of notches in the opposite sides of a plastic storage container, then run your extension cord joints through the container and put the top on. It's a great way to keep your outdoor extension cords dry and safe this holiday season.

247. Hold off as long as possible before buying a tree. The closer you wait to Christmas, the cheaper trees get.

248. Give your tree lights a rustic feel by spray-painting them silver or gold. Just make sure to take the bulbs out first.

249. Putting a small amount of 7UP in a poinsettia's soil will surprisingly preserve it for much longer.

Ten Unique Items to Put on Your Tree Instead of Ornaments

250. Gingerbread men

251. Candy canes

252. Pinecones

253. Photographs

254. Baby mittens or shoes

255. Balls of yarn

256. Christmas cookie cutters

257. Origami doves

258. Miniature wrapped presents

259. Other tree branches or leaves

260. Is your fake Christmas tree looking a little bare after a few years? Slip a couple of wreaths over the top and fluff out the branches. As long as the colors match, it'll look as good as new!

261. Want your fake tree to smell like a real Christmas tree? Light a few pine-scented candles in the same room (just not too close to the tree for safety).

262. Place any bell ornaments on the bottom branches so you can hear if any kids or pets are messing with the tree.

263. Use this handy Christmas tree decorating guide:

If your tree is this tall, use this many ornaments
4 feet: 40–50 ornaments
6 feet: 65–75 ornaments
8 feet: 150–200 ornaments
10 feet: 250–300 ornaments
12 feet: 325–350 ornaments
14 feet: 375–400 ornaments

264. Want to make your tree look like it's covered in snow? Spray it with some artificial snow or SnoFlock. You can buy it online or at most Christmas department stores.

265. Add a white woolly blanket around the base of your tree before you put presents down. This will make it look like they're sitting in a winter wonderland.

266. To make a Christmas book tree, place a small pile of books in the shape of a Christmas tree, then lay some ornaments on a few covers. Voilà! Instant tree!

Chapter 5

Something for the Kids

267. When wrapping gifts for children, make sure all the packaging is removed and batteries (if necessary) are installed.

268. Want to add some magic to a kid's Christmas? Try the Santa's footprints trick: put a pair of boots down by the fireplace and sprinkle sugar or flour around them. Carefully lift off the boots, and you'll be left with some "magical" footprints from the big guy. Kids will never stop believing after seeing these!

269. Make mini elf doughnuts out of Cheerios to go along with Santa's milk and cookies.

270. Is your child worried about how Santa will get in without a chimney? Make a "magical key" and hang it on the door on Christmas Eve.

271. Save yourself some stress on Christmas morning and put together all your kids' gifts that need to be assembled the night before.

272. Kids' winter clothing stink from playing in the snow all day? Spritz it with a solution of ½ cup vinegar mixed with ½ gallon water and hang it to dry. That stinky bacteria will vanish!

273. Use different wrapping paper to easily distinguish which kid's presents are which.

274. Need an easy kid-friendly craft? Make almost any holiday design with some glue and Popsicle sticks: Christmas tree, Santa hat, Star of David, and so on. You can also tie a piece of string to the top for an easy DIY holiday decoration.

275. Ten Kid-Friendly Christmas Movies You Must See

* *A Charlie Brown Christmas*
* *A Christmas Story*
* *Arthur Christmas*
* *How the Grinch Stole Christmas!*
* *The Nightmare Before Christmas*
* *Elf*
* *Miracle on 34th Street*
* *Rudolph the Red-Nosed Reindeer*
* *A Christmas Carol*
* *Home Alone*

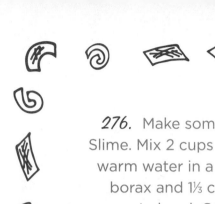

276. Make some kid-approved Snow Slime. Mix 2 cups white glue and 1½ cups warm water in a bowl. Mix ¾ teaspoon borax and 1⅓ cups warm water in a separate bowl. Combine the contents of the bowls. Mix and refrigerate for one hour.

277. Buy the cheapest wrapping paper you can find for your kids' gifts. They really don't care about the presentation. Forget about cards too.

278. Kids' winter boots smelling funky? Use dryer sheets as an incredibly effective shoe deodorizer.

279. Unique gift idea for kids: you can send a picture of your dog to ShelterPups.com, and they'll send you a stuffed animal that looks just like it.

280. Have kids dip some used grape stems into melted chocolate to make some realistic trees for their gingerbread houses.

Ten Ways to Get Kids to Sleep on Christmas Eve

281. Don't let them use cell phones or tablets before bed. Cell phone radiation causes insomnia.

282. Get them active during the day. A little extra playtime or sports will help get them to sleep in a jiffy.

283. Stick to bedtime rituals. Things being just a little "off" before bed can drastically affect sleeping patterns.

284. Try the 4-7-8 technique: four-second inhale, seven-second hold, eight-second release, and repeat. It really works!

285. Taking twenty-minute naps during the day can actually help improve metabolism and the quality of sleep you get during the night.

286. Get them to blink rapidly for sixty seconds. Physically tired eyes will make you fall asleep faster.

287. Play their favorite song. Listening to your favorite song before going to bed makes you fall asleep faster. It also has been found to enhance your mood for the upcoming day.

288. Tell them to count backward from ninety-nine. Chances are they'll be asleep before they get to fifty.

289. Place a warm hot-water bottle in their beds a few minutes before bedtime. There's nothing more soothing than a nice warm bed to get into.

290. If all else fails, go to the good old line of "Santa brings gifts only to kids who are asleep."

291. If your child writes a letter to his favorite Disney character, he can get an 8" × 10" autographed photo. This is a great (almost free) gift idea that kids can do for a sibling or friend too! Here's the address:

ATTN: "Character's name"
Walt Disney World Communications
PO Box 10040
Lake Buena Vista, FL
32830-0040

292. Christmas Eve idea: in Iceland, it's a tradition to exchange your favorite books on Christmas Eve and spend the rest of the night reading and eating chocolate in bed. It's called *Jolabokaflod*, which translates to "Christmas Book Flood."

293. If you bought your kids a gaming system this year, plug it in now and do the updates before you give it to them. That way they won't have to spend one to three hours updating it right when they open it.

294. If your little ones really want to decorate the tree, make them a small one out of felt with felt ornaments to stick on.

295. Make sure you have your kids get all their chores out of the way before you put presents under the tree. This way you can use the idea of getting coal for Christmas to your advantage.

296. Little one all dressed up but missing something? Women's knee-high socks are the perfect size to turn into toddler leggings.

297. Add a festive touch to your kids' lunches by drawing snowmen on cheese-string wrappers with a marker.

298. Want your kids to have perfect smiles in your Christmas photos? Ask them to tell you a joke, but tell them they should absolutely *not* laugh while telling it. This makes for perfect, natural smiles every time.

299. Have kids make their own snow globes with Mason jars, glitter, water, and their own custom centerpieces (toys, ornaments, and action figures work great for this).

300. Change your spouse's name in your phone to Santa and include a Santa profile picture to really get the kids excited on Christmas Eve.

301. Make sure your kids wear sunscreen even in the winter. Just because it's cold out doesn't mean the sun won't impact their skin the same way.

302. Make Christmas even more fun for a little one. Wrap a kid's gift in white paper, tape some crayons onto it, and write the words "color me" on it.

Ten Tips to Winning a Snowball Fight

303. Get to higher ground.
304. Always try to surprise your enemy when you can.
305. Make plenty of ammunition (snowballs) before the fight.
306. Wear gloves, not mittens. Snow tends to stick to mittens, making it harder to build and throw snowballs.
307. Create walls out of tightly packed snow for cover.
308. Always have a home base so your team has a reference point.
309. Infiltrate the enemy base with a spy.
310. Scan your surroundings before the fight. Knowing the battleground beforehand will give you a big advantage.
311. Sometimes base defense is the best offense.
312. White clothing is camouflage in a snowball fight.

313. Here's an inexpensive and fun holiday game for kids: cut out a reindeer face and put it on an old bulletin board. Cut out some red construction paper circles and play Pin the Nose on Rudolph.

314. Kids creating a wrapping paper tornado on Christmas morning? Wrap the biggest cardboard box you can find for a festive garbage bin on Christmas Day.

315. Give your kids a string of lights to play with while taking photos. You'll get the most magical Christmas photos ever!

316. Take your kids' gifts out of those impossible to open plastic packages before you wrap them. It may make the gift harder to wrap neatly, but your kids will get to play with their new toys right away and it'll make for less aggravation for you on Christmas Day.

317. If you have young toddlers, try not to spend a fortune on the "expensive" toys. Sometimes children are more interested in the wrapping paper than the toy itself.

318. A muffin tin makes for the perfect DIY Advent calendar as you can easily find one with twenty-four cups. Simply place a mini treat or toy in each cup, cover each cup with some paper decorated with a number, and hang it up on the wall for your kids to see.

319. Easily help your kids figure out whose gifts are whose by using their photos as gift labels.

320. Easily turn your fridge into a snowman with some felt or construction paper cut into eyes, a carrot nose, a mouth, and even a scarf. Use magnets fastened onto the back to stick the pieces to your fridge. Your kids will be delighted!

321. If the area where you live falls below 32°F this winter, go outside and blow bubbles with your kids. They will magically turn into ice bubbles!

322. Make some Christmas tree cupcakes with your kids! Place an ice cream cone on top of a cupcake, and pipe green frosting all over the cone. Then use edible candies or M&M's for ornaments.

Chapter 6

Go Home for the Holidays

323. Have family flying in? Rather than sift through your local airport's website, simply type the airline and flight number into *Google* to get all the important information you need.

324. The Along the Way app will let you know about any cool attractions you can see on any road trip.

325. Spend more time with your loved ones by getting the SelfControl app. It's a program that blocks sites like *Facebook*, *Twitter*, and email for a specified period of time.

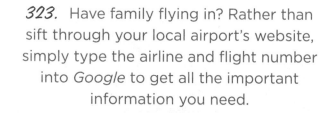

326. When flying somewhere with family this holiday season, make sure to mix up your clothing between the suitcases. That way, if a bag gets lost or stolen, one person isn't totally out of luck.

❋

327. Make two copies of your packing list for your trip. Use one to pack your bag and the second to make sure you bring everything back.

❋

328. Want to be a hero at the airport during the holiday travel rush? Bring a power strip. You'll instantly make a bunch of new friends.

Ten Things You Should Know Before Flying Somewhere for the Holidays

329. Be anonymous: use your browser's incognito tab or delete your history every time you go online to check flight rates. The prices for flights actually go up when you visit a site multiple times.

330. Typically the cheapest time to book a flight is six to eight weeks before you want to travel.

331. The cheapest days to buy tickets are Tuesday and Wednesday.

332. The cheapest days to fly are Tuesday, Wednesday, and Saturday.

333. Booking too early (six months out) can result in paying up to 19 percent more.

334. Sunday is usually the most expensive day to fly.

335. Prices for flights can change up to three times per day.

336. Discount ticket sales are usually offered at the beginning of the week.

337. December 22–29 are the most expensive days to fly.

338. The cheapest days to fly are after Christmas between December 31 and January 5.

339. *Traveling over the holidays? Pack a garbage bag to put your dirty laundry in. You'll never mix up the clean and dirty clothes in your suitcase or backpack again!*

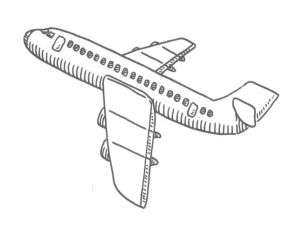

340. The cheapest time to book your holiday flights is December 4–10.

341. Tie a small piece of brightly colored fabric to your luggage. You'll be able to spot your bag at the airport in no time!

342. Making some long-distance calls to relatives this year? Use Google Voice. It's completely free to use, even to landlines!

343. Going on a trip this holiday season? Remember to lock up: do something weird or abnormal when locking your front door so later on you can easily remember that you did it.

344. Before going on your holiday vacation, place a coin on a mug of ice in your freezer. On your return, if the coin is *in* the ice, it means your freezer stopped working at one point and your food has likely gone bad.

345. Come home to a frozen lock? Squirt some hand sanitizer in it. It will unfreeze in seconds.

346. Flying this holiday season? Mark "fragile" on your luggage even if there's nothing fragile in it so your belongings will be handled with care.

347. Keep your car doors from freezing when you're away by applying cooking spray to the cracks of the doors and along the rubber.

Ten Hacks for Your Car When Traveling in the Winter

348. Keep a bag of kitty litter in your trunk. If you ever get stuck in the snow, you can pour the litter under your wheels for traction.

349. Stopping somewhere overnight? Put some socks over your windshield wipers to prevent them from icing up.

350. Make sure to keep up with car washes. Deicing compounds can be corrosive to the surfaces they attach to, like your car's paint.

351. One of the quickest ways to get snow off your vehicle is to use a leaf blower. It works like a charm!

352. Instead of all that grueling scraping on your windshield this winter, try spraying it with a mixture of ⅔ cup vinegar and ⅓ cup water. The ice will melt right off.

353. Want to know if your tires have enough tread to get through your road trip? Stick a penny in the tread. If Lincoln's head shows, you need new tires.

354. DIY windshield washer fluid: 2 quarts rubbing alcohol, 1 cup water, and 1 teaspoon dish detergent.

355. Lock frozen? Use a heat rub, like the kind you would use on a sore muscle. This will loosen the lock almost instantly.

356. Try to park your car overnight facing east. That way the sun will do most of the snow removal for you.

357. Lost or broke your ice scraper while on a road trip? Try using a nonmetal kitchen spatula or a credit card.

358. On a road trip and your car windows keep fogging up on the inside? Wipe them down with some shaving cream. It contains the same ingredients as commercial defoggers.

359. Stop your wiper blades from freezing to your windshield during your road trip by rubbing them with some rubbing alcohol.

360. Car get stuck in the snow while traveling? Turn your floor mats upside down under the wheels that are slipping. This will help give your tires enough traction to get you moving again.

361. Now that you and your family are finally all in the same place, it's time to take that photo for the Christmas cards. Ask the photographer to take a few unannounced pictures as your family gets ready to pose. Sometimes the candid pictures turn out better than posed ones.

362. Spray some WD-40 in your house's keyholes before the winter season arrives. This will prevent them from freezing.

363. You can use toothpaste to clear up your hazy car headlights while you're on the road. Put a blob of toothpaste on a rag or cloth and scrub the headlight. Works like a charm.

364. You don't want to put on stale or stinky clothing for your holiday get-together, so throw a couple of dryer sheets in your suitcase before traveling. Your clothes will smell as fresh as they do when they come out of the dryer.

365. Want to pack a little lighter this year? Try rolling your clothes instead of folding them. This can dramatically cut down the space they take up in your suitcase.

366. Packing jewelry/earrings for your trip? Pack them in some pill containers.

367. Don't want your chargers and cables to be a tangled mess when you get to your destination? Use an old glasses case. They are the perfect size to hold cables, and are built to protect whatever's inside.

368. Want to save space in your suitcase? Stuff your socks and underwear inside your shoes.

369. Always try to ship your gifts
to your destination instead of bringing
them in your suitcase. This frees
up space and is usually cheaper
(depending on the weight), and you don't
run the risk of them being
confiscated at customs.

370. You'll need to be clean shaven
for all those holiday parties, so put a
binder clip over the head of your razor to
protect it while traveling.

371. Got a bunch of leftover change on
your last day of Christmas vacation?
It's usually not worth bringing back
and exchanging at a bank. Give it to a
homeless person.

372. Want to make sure your nice
Christmas shoes stay squeaky
clean in your suitcase? Put them inside
a shower cap.

373. Always make sure to take a photo
of your luggage before setting out on
your holiday travels. This will help speed
up the paperwork process immensely if
your luggage gets lost.

374. Never get your necklace tangled
in your suitcase again by feeding
one end through a straw and then
clasping it closed.

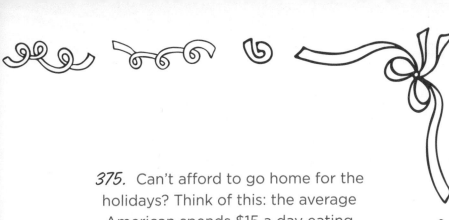

375. Can't afford to go home for the holidays? Think of this: the average American spends $15 a day eating out. That's $450 a month, $600–$750 including drinks. If you stop eating out for two months or so, you could buy a ticket to travel anywhere in the world.

376. Put everyone's sleepwear and toothbrushes in one easy-to-reach bag. That way when you get to your destination, you won't have to fumble through a bunch of suitcases on the first night.

377. Don't want your bobby pins ending up all over your suitcase? Use a Tic Tac container. They hold pins perfectly, and make it super easy to get one out when you need one.

378. Buying all those mini travel containers of toothpaste, mouthwash, hand sanitizer, and so on can get expensive. Stop buying them and just refill old ones with big bottles at home.

379. The holidays are expensive enough, so stop buying water bottles on the plane. Bring an empty one and just fill it up once you get past security.

Chapter 7

Holiday Remedies

380. Have a holiday stress headache? Eating ten to twelve almonds is the equivalent of taking two aspirins for a migraine headache.

381. No one wants to be coughing all through the holidays. Get rid of nighttime coughs by putting Vicks VapoRub on your feet and then placing socks over them. Your cough will stop within minutes.

382. To cure a sore throat, add a teaspoon of honey to Jell-O mix and heat it up. The gelatin will coat and soothe your throat.

383. Got a stomachache from eating too many holiday goodies? Hop in the shower and let the water hit your body for fifteen to twenty minutes. Your aching will go away and won't come back!

384. How do you get rid of those bags under your eyes that you got from staying up too late wrapping presents? Get a raw potato, wash it, and peel it. Cut two slices off and place them directly under your eyes. Relax for a few minutes.

Ten Teas to Try When the Holidays Have Given You...

385. A headache = Ginger tea

386. Bad breath = Black tea

387. The jitters = Passionflower tea

388. Allergy sniffles = Nettle tea

389. 3 p.m. cravings = Green tea

390. A holiday daze = Ginkgo tea

391. Not enough sleep = Valerian tea

392. A sweet tooth = Licorice tea

393. Belly woes = Peppermint tea

394. The need for a faster calorie burn = Oolong tea

395. Lose your voice from all that holiday fun? Gargle 1 teaspoon Tabasco sauce mixed in a glass of water. The capsaicin from the peppers curbs inflammation in the vocal cords.

396. Get dry or cracked fingers in the winter? Use some ChapStick on them to get rid of those small cuts.

397. Holiday hangover? According to a study, smelling rubbing alcohol can relieve nausea almost instantly.

398. Have chapped winter lips? Put a water-soaked green tea bag on your lips for five minutes. Problem solved!

399. Need to go outside for a long period of time this winter? Slick some antiperspirant deodorant onto your feet. It will keep your feet warm and prevent blisters.

400. Got the sniffles and don't want to be stuck holding all those gross used tissues all day long? Take an empty tissue box and attach it to a full tissue box with elastic bands. Now you've got a portable trash can! Put your used tissues in the empty box and throw it away when it's full.

✳

401. No time for a runny or stuffy nose this holiday? Push your tongue against the roof of your mouth and push a finger between your eyebrows. Hold it for about twenty seconds. Your nose should clear.

402. Coughing and no time to run out to a store? The most effective cough syrup that exists is honey, which you probably have in your cabinet at this moment.

403. Burn yourself while cooking that holiday meal? Either mustard or toothpaste applied topically will help ease the pain of minor burns.

404. Have a stomachache from all that food? Lie on your left side and rub your stomach in clockwise circles. It actually helps!

405. Keep your clothes looking good for all those holiday parties. Put clear nail polish onto the outer threads of a button to keep it from unraveling or popping off your jacket or sweater.

406. Boots get soaked in a snowstorm? Stuff them with crumpled newspapers and put them in front of your fridge, and they'll dry in a few hours.

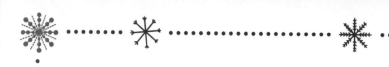

407. Salt stains on your shoes? Wipe them with a cloth dipped in a solution of 1 tablespoon vinegar and 1 cup water. Boom! Stains gone!

408. Too busy with holiday preparations to run to the drugstore? Before the holiday season starts, put together a "sick kit" for those times you get sick and don't want to/can't make it to the store.

409. Stuffy nose? Leave a sliced onion near where you sleep and let it sit for the night. Your nose will be clear by the time you wake up.

410. Have a pounding migraine headache from all that holiday shopping? Try eating spinach instead of popping a pill. Magnesium is used in the ER to treat migraine attacks, and spinach contains loads of magnesium, as well as riboflavin, another aid in reducing migraine attacks.

Ten Things to Take When You Get That Holiday Cold/Flu

411. **Grapefruit seed extract:** Put five to fifteen drops in a cup of fruit juice. This has been known to boost your immune system. Do not use when breastfeeding!

412. **Catnip tea:** This tea is not for cats. It stops the sick sweats and helps you get into that deep sleep cycle.

413. **Tea tree oil:** Place a drop on your finger and suck it off. Swish it around your mouth and then spit out. Great for easing a sore throat or headache.

414. **Hot salt water:** Gargling an 8-ounce glass of hot water with ¼–½ teaspoon salt mixed in three or four times a day will help relieve pain from a swollen throat.

415. **Apple cider vinegar:** Sip a glass of hot water with 2 tablespoons apple cider vinegar and 1 tablespoon raw honey mixed in. This helps your body fight infection and will cut through any phlegm in your throat.

416. **Activated charcoal pills:** These pills bind toxins and sickness-causing germs in your digestive system.

417. **Detox bath:** Mix 2 cups Epsom salt, ¼ cup grated ginger, and six to eight drops eucalyptus oil into a hot bath (as hot as you can stand).

418. **Gingerroot:** A spoonful of this stuff will take care of any nausea. It's best to take it after a meal because it can be acidic in your stomach.

419. **Peppermint oil:** Rub five drops onto the bottom of each foot. This will reduce any fever you have.

420. **Coconut oil:** Mix a scoop into your food or tea to help strengthen your immune system and deter illness.

421. Need to cool down your body temperature? Run your wrist under cold water for at least five minutes. It'll cool your blood down.

422. A perfect holiday headache remedy that will rehydrate you and flush toxins out of your body: mix 3 mint leaves, ½ cucumber sliced, ½ lemon sliced, and 1 cup filtered water. Drink two or three times a day when you have a headache.

423. Drinking one glass of grape juice can relieve migraine headaches almost instantly.

424. Feel the urge to vomit but have a houseful of guests? You can stop yourself by eating a mint or chewing minty gum.

425. Holiday hot sauce remedy for a cold: mix fresh sliced ginger, a squeeze of lemon juice, a squirt or two of sriracha sauce, and a cup of hot water.

426. Some relative get a little tipsy and spill wine on your carpet? It may sound crazy, but white wine will actually take out a red wine stain.

427. Christmas sweater got that annoying static cling? Put a safety pin in it. The static will instantly go away.

428. Got a pounding headache that just won't go away? Take a lime, cut it in half, and rub it on your forehead. The throbbing should go away.

429. Drinking two glasses of Gatorade can relieve headache pain almost immediately, without the unpleasant side effects caused by traditional pain relievers.

430. Have a headache? Submerge your feet and hands in hot water and put a bag of frozen peas on the back of your head. The heat on your extremities pulls the blood from your head, relieving your head pains.

431. Have a sore throat? Try eating a piece of cucumber. It cools down your throat and stops that itchy feeling.

432. Have a headache? Eat a mint leaf. Mint has also been proven to reduce your stress levels.

433. In the middle of your holiday party when you start coughing uncontrollably? Try raising your hands above your head, and the coughing will stop.

434. Not getting enough sleep over the holiday season? Simply believing you've slept well, even if you haven't, will improve your day's performance and mental alertness.

435. Pineapple juice is five times more effective than cough syrup. It also prevents colds and the flu.

436. Try this sickness prevention tea to stay healthy this holiday season: 2 tablespoons honey, 2 tablespoons vinegar, a dash of cinnamon, and 2 tablespoons lemon juice. Mix well and drink.

437. *Upset stomach this holiday? Try these ten foods that can get rid of it:*

* Bananas
* Ginger
* Plain yogurt
* Papaya
* Applesauce
* Oatmeal
* White rice
* Chamomile tea
* Chicken broth
* Aloe vera juice

Ten Ways to Prevent Yourself from Getting a Cold This Holiday Season

438. Stop touching your nose and eyes.

439. Exercise on a regular basis.

440. Eat fresh fruits and veggies to support your immune system.

441. Make sure to wash your hands every time you shake someone else's.

442. Stay as far away from sick people as possible.

443. Don't skimp on sleep.

444. Stop biting your nails.

445. Stay as hydrated as possible.

446. Don't share food or drinks with people.

447. Smile more. A simple smile has been proven to boost your immune system.

Chapter 8

Emergency Holiday De-Stress

448. Holidays got you riled up? Try eating 1 cup of low-fat yogurt or 2 tablespoons of mixed nuts. The amino acids in these foods will help you calm down.

449. Watermelon can help relieve stress and anxiety, keep you energized, and boost your metabolism.

450. Here's a mindful breathing technique to calm the holiday craziness that you can do anywhere: inhale for six seconds; hold your breath for seven seconds; exhale for eight seconds.

451. Try to stretch for a solid five to ten minutes each day this holiday season. Most people spend the majority of their day sitting or lying down, which causes muscles to tense up, producing that feeling of stress/anxiety.

❄

452. The start of your day can have repercussions on the rest of it. Before you do anything, take ten minutes to sit and relax in silence. This will set a nice, calming tone for the rest of the day.

453. There's nothing better for stress than running. Outside of meditation, it's one of the best ways to clear your mind. If it's too cold outside this holiday, try running on a treadmill.

454. Hang some eucalyptus around your showerhead. The steam will release an amazing fragrance and beneficial oils every time you shower.

Easy Activities to Get Rid of Holiday Anxiety

455. On a piece of paper, write down a list of your skills. Read that list two or three times a day.

456. Do some yoga poses and meditate.

457. Exercise. It is proven to increase your endorphin levels.

458. Pinpoint areas of stress in your life and figure out how to change them.

459. Visit an alternative-healing practitioner.

460. Spend time with people you enjoy being around—it is the holidays after all!

461. Set a daily routine.

462. Stop avoiding things out of fear.

463. Practice affirmations.

464. Squeeze the fleshy place between your index finger and your thumb known as the Hoku point in traditional Chinese medicine. Applying firm pressure there for just thirty seconds can reduce tension and stress in your upper body.

465. Avocados boost serotonin levels. Eating them is a good way to improve your mood and relieve depression.

466. One of the biggest reasons people are grumpy around the winter holidays is because they lack vitamin D. In the summer you get it naturally from being outside in the sun, but you can replicate this by taking a daily vitamin D pill.

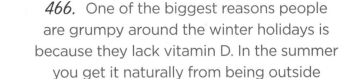

467. Belt out those carols! Singing releases a large number of endorphins in your brain and can make you feel better almost instantly.

468. Drink a tall glass of cold water when you're feeling stressed. Your problem could be dehydration, not stress.

469. Had a stressful day? Take some time at night to think of three things that actually went right. It may be hard at first, but ending the day with a small positive thought sets you up for a positive tomorrow.

470. Indulge in some chocolate. There's no shortage of it this time of year, and it contains phenylethylamine and tryptophan, which release serotonin (your body's natural "happy drug") to your brain.

471. Surrounding yourself with nature has been associated with increased vitality. So go make a snowman, take some pictures, or just go for a walk. It will help.

472. Eating a banana can actually help your mind relax, making you feel happier and stress-free!

Ten Quick Ways to De-Stress in Sixty Seconds

473. Go outside

474. Chew a piece of gum

475. Squeeze a stress ball

476. Do twenty jumping jacks

477. Spend some time with your pets

478. Punch a pillow

479. Listen to your favorite song

480. Take a shower

481. Doodle or draw something

482. Call a friend

483. Simple detox bath: drop five to ten green tea bags in your bath while the water is running. This will relax your body and give your skin ample minerals.

484. Yawning actually cools down your brain, which helps get rid of stress. Can't yawn? Think of the word *yawn* or watch a video of someone yawning.

485. Make a holiday to-do list. Simply getting the tasks you need to finish out of your head and onto a sheet of paper will make you feel a lot less stressed.

486. Sleep and stress go hand in hand. Make sure you're at least getting seven solid hours of sleep a night.

487. Holiday plans getting to be too much? Distract yourself. Do something that will take your mind away for fifteen minutes. Play a musical instrument, do some knitting, paint a picture, and so on.

488. Lie on the ground faceup with your back against the floor and your legs against the wall at a 90-degree angle. Holding this pose for five minutes will eliminate any stress or headaches you may have.

489. *Holiday panic attack relief:*

* Sit down and try to relax all the muscles in your body.
* Breathe in deeply through your nose, and out slowly through your mouth.
* While doing this, close your eyes and focus your mind on the word "calm."
* Repeat until the panic attack subsides.

490. Smiling for sixty seconds, even when you're in a bad mood, will immediately improve your mood. Using these muscles is enough to trigger the happy chemicals in your brain.

491. Frazzled by all the holiday hubbub? Chew some gum. A 2008 study showed that chewing gum reduces levels of cortisol (a stress hormone) in your body.

492. Cut yourself off from technology for a few hours. No phones, laptops, desktop computers, or TV. No bad news, obligations, or people nagging you can really lift your mood.

493. A 2007 study found that drinking hot chocolate increases the blood flow to key areas of the brain, boosting alertness and increasing performance for two to three hours. So drink up!

494. The website www.donothingfor2minutes.com (you need to have "www." in front of it) is a simple challenge where you just have to sit, do nothing, and look at a beautiful sunset for two minutes. Try it this holiday for some much-needed holiday stress relief.

495. Once a week over the holiday season, try this de-stress bath: a hot bath (as hot as you can bear) with a handful of Epsom salt, ten drops of lavender essential oil, and ½ cup baking soda.

496. Want to feel better instantly? Snuggle, hug, or kiss someone you love. It may seem obvious, but it also has been scientifically proven to lower blood pressure.

497. Do a little dance. Lock the door and let loose. Researchers at the University of Texas at Austin say that a single forty-minute exercise session can immediately boost your mood.

498. Aromatherapy can be a great way to relieve stress. The scent of lavender has been shown to reduce stress levels.

499. The holidays are a perfect time to start a gratitude journal. Whenever you're stressed, write down things you're thankful for. You'll be surprised at how well this works.

500. Try to stick to a daily routine this holiday season. Christmas duties can put you far away from your daily routine, but keeping a few things like reading before bed, going to the gym in the morning, or having an afternoon nap can keep your stress levels at bay.

501. Find some happy this holiday by sniffing some lemons. According to researchers at The Ohio State University, simply smelling the citrusy fragrance can instantly improve your mood.

502. When the holiday stress becomes too much to handle, let out your stress the old-fashioned way with a good yell. Seriously, go to a quiet place or drive somewhere no one will hear you, and just let it all out.

Chapter 9

Holiday Parties

503. Use frozen grapes to cool down your wine without having to water it down.

504. Need a ride home on New Year's Eve? Call AAA at 1-800-AAA-HELP (1-800-222-4357). They will pick anyone up and drive them home free of charge.

505. Need an easy way to clear your walkways so your guests don't take a spill? Mix 1 teaspoon liquid dish soap, 1 tablespoon rubbing alcohol, and ½–1 gallon water and pour it over your walkways. It will clear the ice and snow without refreezing.

506. Want some toasty legs while you're out shoveling the snow before your guests arrive? Wear running tights instead of long johns. They breathe more, hold less moisture, and feel way better as a base layer.

507. Make a festive cocktail by filling a glass with cotton candy and pouring in some champagne. You can use Perrier carbonated mineral water for a nonalcoholic version.

508. No corkscrew for your wine bottle? Hammer a nail into the top of the cork, and pry the nail out with the hammer's reverse side. The nail will pop right out with the cork attached.

509. Has your New Year's Eve champagne gone flat? Drop a raisin in and watch the bubbles magically return.

510. Holding your drink at belly button level at holiday parties will make you look more confident.

511. Tired of getting wet socks while shoveling the driveway before your guests arrive? Slip a couple of sandwich bags over your feet before you put your boots on.

512. Feet freezing cold after shoveling for your guests? Cut out wool insoles and glue them to your shoe insoles for extra warmth.

513. Entertain your guests with an awesome visualizer by hitting Command + T while a song is playing in iTunes.

Ten Christmas Party Snack Ideas

514. **Marshmallow Snowmen:** Stack three different-sized marshmallows on top of each other, use two pretzel sticks for arms, chocolate icing for facial features, and a piece of licorice for a scarf.

515. **Pita Christmas Trees:** Cut triangular pieces of pita bread, smear them with guacamole, and use cut veggies for the decorations.

516. **Cheese String Snowmen:** Use a marker to draw snowman features on packages of white cheese strings. This is perfect for making your kids' lunches a little more festive.

517. **Festive Jell-O Shots:** Make red, white, and green Jell-O packages. Mix in one shot vodka. Pour and freeze one layer at a time while alternating colors. They end up looking like candy canes!

518. **Grinch Kabobs:** Put a mini marshmallow, a strawberry, a banana slice, and a grape (in that order) on a skewer. It'll look just like the Grinch.

519. **Fruit and Cheese Christmas Tree:** Layer different cheeses and grapes in a half-diamond shape. Use a celery stalk for the base of the tree.

520. **Eggnog Shooters:** Turn ketchup cups into perfect eggnog shooters.

521. **Snowman Dip:** Turn any dip bowl into a snowman face by adding a few black olives for eyes and a mouth, and a carrot for the nose.

522. **Pizza Stocking:** Cut out some pizza dough in the shape of a stocking. Use pizza sauce for the base and a line of cheese at the top for the frilly white bit.

523. **Babybel Santa Faces:** Take off the bottom half of a Babybel wax wrapper, dip the exposed cheese half in cream cheese to make a beard, and use a food marker to add facial features on the remainder of the cheese.

524. Freeze red, white, and green water balloons, and put them around your drinks in a cooler or bucket. This cools down your beverages at a party with a more festive and less drippy effect.

525. Melt any kind of chocolate for your guests in a Mason jar that is set in your slow cooker. Put the slow cooker on a low setting so the topping stays warm and gooey for your guests.

526. Make your balloons more festive by placing red and green glow sticks in them before blowing them up.

527. Put a few glow sticks in the drink cooler or bucket for easy drink grabbing without needing a flashlight.

528. Before your guests arrive, wrap rubber bands around the ends of coat hangers to prevent coats from slipping off.

529. Your iPhone pictures of your party will be of better quality if you take the picture and then zoom in on the saved version rather than zooming in while taking the picture.

530. Serving Christmas cookies at your party? Stack them in a triangular shape, sprinkle powdered sugar on them, and put a star on top. You have yourself a Christmas cookie tree.

531. Want to know if you have bad breath when you need to talk to people at your party? Lick your wrist and smell it. This is what your breath smells like to others.

532. Guest drop a wineglass? Pick up every little shard of glass with a piece of bread.

533. Have better-tasting chips at your party: open the bag from the bottom, where all the flavor sinks.

534. Try this Christmas drinking game: put a Santa hat on the corner of your TV. Every time someone on TV looks like they're wearing the hat, you drink.

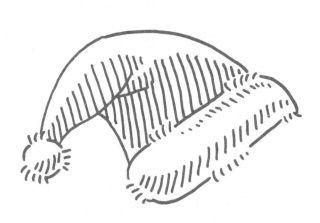

535. Sound system not working? Toss your phone into an empty flower vase and play the music on it.

536. Got an ugly Christmas sweater party to go to? Tape a mirror on any old sweater. Boom. Ugliest sweater of them all!

537. Scoop your ice cream and store it in the freezer to speed up the dessert serving process at your party.

538. Mixing alcohol with Diet Coke will get you drunker than if you mix it with regular Coke.

539. Always hold your drink in your left hand at parties. That way, your right hand won't be cold or wet when you shake someone's hand.

540. Never take ibuprofen on an empty stomach to cure your party hangover. It can actually tear your stomach lining.

541. A wineglass set in a large bowl makes for a great chip 'n' dip set.

542. Plan your transportation for New Year's Eve before you go out to avoid the hassle of looking for a cab when you need one.

543. No need to throw those stale leftover chips into the trash. Simply heat them in the oven for two minutes. They'll taste as good as new!

544. Run out of places to keep drinks cold at a party? Put some ice in the washing machine and use it as an extra cooler.

545. Buy the alcohol for your party at a warehouse (or wholesale) club. You don't need a membership, and it's usually 25–35 percent off. It's great for when you're hosting a party, but keep in mind that you may have to do a little persuading with the card checker employee if they're unaware of this policy.

546. Need some quick decorations for your party? Cut some white coffee filters into snowflakes.

Ways to Cure (or Avoid) a Holiday Party Hangover

547. Try honey on crackers. The fructose in the honey will help flush out the alcohol in your system.

548. Soaking your feet in hot water will help your head feel better.

549. Drink sports drinks. They have excellent hydrating agents.

550. Eat a big, greasy meal before you start drinking. Grease lines your stomach and prepares it for the night's battle.

551. Drink one glass of water for every alcoholic drink you have, and you'll get drunk without getting a hangover.

552. Eat some toast. Toast will bring your blood sugar levels back up to normal after a hard night on your liver.

553. Drink lighter beer. The darker the color of the alcohol you're drinking, the worse your hangover will be.

554. Go for a walk, run, or swim. Although it may not be fun at first, exercise will release endorphins and improve your mood.

555. Drink water with an Alka-Seltzer.

556. Bananas help relieve headaches, depression, and cramps. Perfect for a hangover!

557. Drink Pedialyte, the children's fruit-flavored drink for dehydration. It's designed to replenish and rehydrate your body with electrolytes and has been known to work wonders. It also comes in an ice pop form.

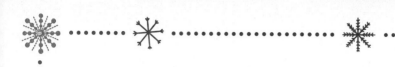

558. Cut up pool noodles and put them in your guests' boots. The noodles will prevent the boots from flopping over and creating a winter boot graveyard.

559. Create festive ice cubes by freezing cranberries in an ice cube tray. Not only are cranberries the fruit of the holiday season, but they look beautiful floating in a glass.

560. Making Jell-O shots for your party? Stack them in a triangular shape and throw a star on top for your very own Christmas Jell-O shot tree.

561. No more room for drinks in the fridge? Put a garbage bag with ice inside a beer or soda case to create a disposable cooler.

562. When sending guests directions to your house, don't just send them the address; send them a picture of your house too. This will make it way easier for them to find it instead of searching up and down the street for house numbers.

563. Use an old bar cart to set up a make-your-own-hot-chocolate bar with all the yummy essentials.

564. Sprucing up your house for guests? Use the thirty-minute rule: if something takes longer than thirty minutes to do, cross it off your list. The goal is to spiff up the place, not turn it into a work of art.

565. Always make sure to tire your pets out before your guests arrive. You can thank me later for that one.

566. No helium to fill your balloons for your Christmas party? Just put vinegar and baking soda in a bottle, and then attach the balloons to the top of the bottle.

Chapter 10

Shedding the Holiday Pounds

567. Drinking 2 cups of water before meals can make you lose an average of 4½ more pounds in twelve weeks.

568. The faster you eat, the more weight you gain. A study showed that fast eaters gained more than 4 pounds over eight years, while slow eaters gained only 1½ pounds.

569. Doing 7,000 jumping jacks burns enough calories to lose about 1 pound. Spread that over a week, and you'll lose an extra pound every week.

570. A big part of losing weight is cutting down on alcoholic beverages. A beer is 150 calories, a glass of wine is 100 calories, and spirits are roughly 105 calories. So try a dry January to shed some holiday pounds.

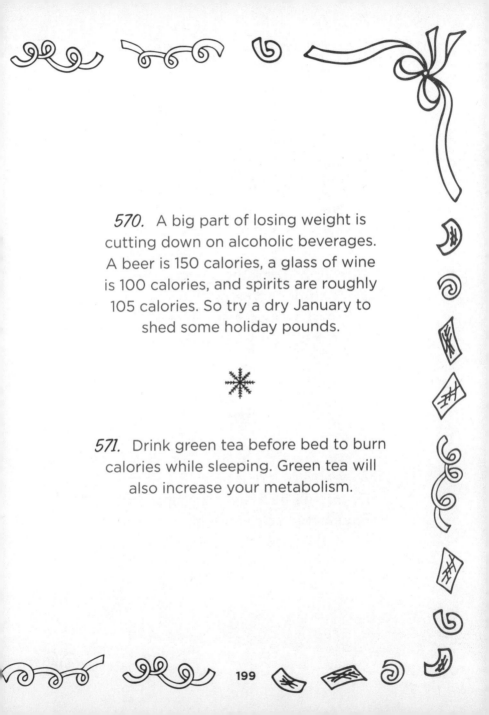

571. Drink green tea before bed to burn calories while sleeping. Green tea will also increase your metabolism.

Five Simple Ways to Shed Holiday Pounds

572. Drink more water.

573. Adjust your portion sizes.

574. Lower your sugar intake.

575. Eat fewer carbs.

576. Don't eat fast food.

577. Want to burn a quick 100 calories?
Do twenty push-ups, fifteen squats,
fifty jumping jacks, and thirty crunches!
Repeat three times.

578. Running in the morning before you eat breakfast is better for weight loss, while running midafternoon is better for building your speed and endurance.

579. Can't find time to exercise? Make it a habit to do twenty-five jumping jacks every time you come out of the bathroom. It won't take any real time from your day, but it will greatly improve your health.

580. The scent of a banana contains a compound that may actually help you lose weight.

581. *Ten Foods That Burn Belly Fat*
* Oatmeal
* Almonds
* Olive oil
* Eggs
* Whey protein
* Berries
* Lean meats
* Whole grains
* Peanut butter
* Green veggies

582. Eating a spoonful of peanut butter before bed helps you burn more calories while you sleep.

583. Drinking 5 cups of green tea in a day can help you lose weight around your belly.

584. Try this morning detox drink: 1 cup warm water, 2 tablespoons apple cider vinegar, 2 tablespoons lemon juice, 1 tablespoon raw honey, 1 teaspoon cinnamon, and a dash of cayenne. Mix and drink before breakfast.

585. Need some motivation to go to the gym after the holidays? Pact is an app that will pay you for working out and punishes you for missing out on days.

586. You can burn up to 180 calories while watching a horror movie.

587. Dieting tip: treat soda like it's candy, not a drink. Most sodas and candy have almost equal amounts of sugar.

588. Looking to lose holiday weight? Keep these stats in mind as you have your meals:

* To lose 0.1 pound, you have to burn 350 calories.
* To lose 0.2 pound, you have to burn 700 calories.
* To lose 0.3 pound, you have to burn 1,050 calories.
* To lose 0.4 pound, you have to burn 1,400 calories.
* To lose 0.5 pound, you have to burn 1,750 calories.
* To lose 0.6 pound, you have to burn 2,100 calories.
* To lose 0.7 pound, you have to burn 2,450 calories.
* To lose 0.8 pound, you have to burn 2,800 calories.
* To lose 0.9 pound, you have to burn 3,150 calories.
* To lose 1.0 pound, you have to burn 3,500 calories.

589. Want to lose weight? Don't eat dinner within four hours of going to bed. It really makes a huge difference.

590. *Five Drinks That Can Help You Lose Weight*

* Water
* Unsweetened tea
* Skim milk
* Black coffee
* Vegetable juice

591. To lose a pound of fat, you must run for more than three hours. Run for twenty-seven minutes a day, and lose a pound a week.

592. Eating breakfast in the morning makes it ten times easier to burn calories throughout the day.

593. Skipping is one of the most effective forms of cardio. Simply doing ten to fifteen minutes of skipping can burn more than 200 calories.

594. Want to lose weight? Eat spicy foods. Spicy foods trick your taste buds into being more satisfied with smaller amounts of food.

595. Burn 100 calories right now: do forty jumping jacks, thirty crunches, twenty squats, and ten push-ups.

596. Trying to eat less? Use a smaller plate. It tricks your mind into thinking there's more food and limits what you can pile onto your plate.

597. Clean up your diet in five weeks by doing the following:

* **Week 1:** Add real, whole fruits and veggies to every meal.
* **Week 2:** Stop eating fast food.
* **Week 3:** Give up white bread and grains. Switch to wheat bread, brown rice, and whole wheat pasta.
* **Week 4:** Use a fruit or veggie as the base of every snack.
* **Week 5:** Stop drinking soda and sugary drinks.

598. After the holidays are over, there's no excuse to have big amounts of sugar and flour in your diet. Cutting down on both of these is a key component to healthy weight loss.

599. Drinking cold water will help you lose weight naturally and speeds up your metabolism.

600. Dieting tip: don't eat till you are full; eat till you're not hungry anymore.

601. Ten Healthy (and Just As Delicious) Substitutes for Not So Healthy Foods

* Instead of white rice = Quinoa

* Instead of French fries = Sweet potato fries

* Instead of tomato sauce = Freshly diced tomatoes

* Instead of fruit juice = Fruit water

* Instead of sliced bread = Pita bread

* Instead of sour cream = Greek yogurt

* Instead of mashed potatoes = Mashed cauliflower

* Instead of mayonnaise = Mashed avocado

* Instead of pasta = Wheat pasta

* Instead of flour tortilla = Corn tortilla

602. Drink one glass of cold water every hour that you're awake. This will dramatically flush out bad toxins in your body, helping you shed some pounds.

603. You don't need to go to the gym to get a full-body workout. Try these at-home exercises to work your whole body:

* 20 sit-ups
* 15 push-ups
* 20 arm circles
* 30 calf raises
* 30-second plank
* 15 frog jumps
* 20 squats
* 20-second wall sit

604. Make sure you're getting at least six hours of sleep every night. Getting less than that can lower your metabolism by 15 percent.

605. Work on having good posture. By simply having better posture, your body is able to burn 10 percent more calories.

606. Losing weight doesn't always mean dieting and going to the gym. Although these are great, try finding something you love to do that burns calories, like hiking, playing tennis, golfing, swimming, cycling, or other sports.

607. The ultimate detox water: ½ cucumber sliced, 1 lime slice, 1 sprig of mint leaves, and a standard glass of water.

608. Make a New Year's resolution to start running? Here are six tips for new runners:

* When starting out, make sure to focus solely on form. Keep your hips, spine, and neck aligned when running.

* Get some new sneakers; wearing your old worn-out pair will not lead to success.

* Try run/walk intervals at first.

* Stay hydrated.

* Remember to take rest days.

* Keep your goals simple, and reward yourself when you reach them.

Chapter 11

The Holiday
Aftermath

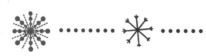

609. Fold your receipt around your gift card after you use it so that you always know your balance.

610. Use egg cartons to store your smaller ornaments. They are the perfect size, provide extra support, and are stackable.

611. Wrap your Christmas lights around a hanger to prevent them from getting tangled.

612. If you have a gift card with less than $10 on it, the business is legally required to give you the rest of your balance in cash.

613. Store your fragile ornaments in old coffee containers stuffed with newspaper.

614. Sick of having a box of tangled Christmas lights every year? Wrap them around paper towel rolls to organize them.

Ten Things You Can Buy Cheap after the Holidays

615. **Holiday decorations:** Big box stores always have big clearance sales the week after Christmas. You can save a few bucks on next year.

616. **TVs:** Due to the fact that TVs are a big seller at the start of the holidays, they always seem to drastically drop in price the week after Christmas.

617. **Exercise equipment:** Since January is the month of resolutions, fitness retailers usually have huge sales after the holiday season to entice buyers.

618. **Cars:** At the end of the model year, dealerships are always eager to get their old cars off the lot.

619. **Gift sets:** Not usually the greatest sellers come holiday time, but if you can find the right combo of items, you can snag a big deal.

620. **Winter coats:** Clothing stores always want to get rid of their winter inventory to make way for spring.

621. **Wrapping paper:** There's no need for stores to keep Christmas wrapping paper until next year. Save a few bucks and buy yours a year early.

622. **Food:** Look for holiday treats like baking mixes, candy, hot chocolate, Christmas-inspired coffee flavors, or basically any food in red and green packaging.

623. **Baking supplies:** If you don't mind a little festive flair on your packaging, you can scoop up some sweet deals.

624. **Candles:** Same goes with candles. You can get some great deals on red and green candles.

625. Add a tablespoon of coarse salt while washing your holiday meal pots and pans to make sure you get all the grease and grime out.

626. Nails dry and brittle from the cold winter months? Paint them with olive oil and sleep with cotton gloves on.

627. Want your kitchen appliances to look like they did at the start of the holidays? Mix ¼ cup baking soda in a bowl with enough peroxide to turn it into a paste. Rub this on any kitchen appliance (stove, oven, pans, fridge door handles, and so on) to make it spotless!

628. When cleaning up after Christmas, try following the "get one, give one" rule: for every item you received as a gift, try to throw out or donate an old one. This will keep your house at the same clutter level.

629. Don't leave the empty boxes from the expensive electronics you got on the curb after Christmas (or any time) as it's an invite for a thief.

630. Lemon water can help clean all the toxins out of your body after the holidays. When you get rid of toxic waste in your system, your skin will be the first to show it.

631. Sick of pine needles getting everywhere when you dispose of your tree? Wrap some trash bags around it before you drag it out. Just make sure to remove them once you get it to the curb, or it will be taken to the dump and not mulched.

632. Scared you'll forget about gift cards you received as gifts? On your iPhone, go to the Reminders app, then hit "Remind me at location" of wherever your gift card works.

633. Keep your old candy/chocolate boxes from the holidays. They make perfect ornament storage boxes.

634. Do you put off unpacking after a holiday trip? Make your first step dumping the entire suitcase onto your bed. Want to sleep? Better put your stuff away.

635. Place a file label over your gift cards and write down your current balance on it.

636. You can repurpose old wrapping paper rolls by wrapping your used tinsel or garland around them. This will keep them in usable shape for next year.

637. Need to exchange an unused item but don't have a receipt? Tell the store that you received it as a gift without a receipt.

638. Use some of those leftover red Solo cups from your party to put your decorations away safely. Simply mount the cups onto a large piece of cardboard, put in your ornaments and some tissue or newspaper to prevent breakage, and stack the cardboard sheets on top of each other in a storage container.

639. Start the new year with an empty jar and fill it with good things that happen. Every time something good happens, write it on a piece of paper and put it in the jar. On the following New Year's Eve, empty it to see all the awesome stuff that happened.

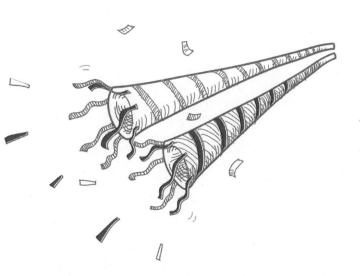

640. Did you get a bunch of gift cards you don't want? You can sell them or exchange them on gift card resale websites like GiftCardGranny.com.

641. Always start from the bottom when taking lights off your Christmas tree. This will prevent tangling, and you can wrap them directly into storage.

642. Write down the serial numbers of any expensive gifts you received. If one gets stolen, it's much easier to prove that the item is yours if it's found.

643. Wrap your Christmas lights around a square piece of cardboard for easy, tangle-free storage.

644. Use all the Christmas cards you received this year to get some perfect contact photos for your phone.

645. Starting on the first day of January, try doing this for twenty-one days: no candy, no cakes, no chips, no white bread, no fast food, no chocolate, no ice cream. The results are incredible!

Ten Tips to Make Your New Year's Resolutions Stick

646. Keep it simple. Sometimes people go too big for their New Year's resolution. A "baby steps" approach where you start small will yield better results.

647. Be realistic. Know your limitations and set goals you think will be tough but are manageable. Making $3 million this month might be setting yourself up for failure.

648. Choose one or two resolutions max. There's nothing worse than having fifteen resolutions to deal with on January 1.

649. The fourth Friday of January is known as "Fail Friday." It's statistically the day when most people will give up on their New Year's resolutions. Beat the odds and stay strong.

650. Make a list of pros and cons. Seeing the benefits of your resolution on paper will help keep you motivated.

651. Tell everyone. Telling people your resolution will give you motivation out of the sheer embarrassment of having to tell them you failed.

652. Reward yourself. When you reach milestones in your resolution, treat yourself to something—as long as it doesn't contradict your resolution.

653. Do it for twenty-one days. Experts say it takes twenty-one days to develop a new habit. Get yourself to this milestone, and things will become much easier.

654. Ask for help. Friends or family already achieved what you want? Reach out to them. You'd be surprised at how much people like to help others better themselves.

655. Don't beat yourself up. The occasional slip of your resolution doesn't mean all is lost. Do the best you can each day, and take things one day at a time.

656. Baking soda can clean appliances, bathtubs, carpets, dishes, counters, drains, floors, grout, laundry, marble, pots and pans, and pretty much any stain.

657. Cleaning out your room, home, or garage after the holidays? Don't tell yourself "I could use this" as a reason for keeping something. Ask yourself, "*Will* I use this?"

658. Start a new tradition that lets Santa Claus take back toys your kids don't use anymore.

659. Pay attention to the smell of your home when you come back from your holiday trip. That's what it smells like to guests all the time; you've just gotten used to it.

660. Make your kitchen smell nice in five seconds: throw an ice cube and a fresh mint leaf into the garbage disposal and turn it on.

Ten Things to Do with a Gift You Don't Want

661. Ask for the receipt and simply return it for the cash.
662. Donate it to charity.
663. Give it as a gift to someone else.
664. Use it for a game of Yankee Swap.
665. Sell it on an auction site like *eBay*.
666. If it's a gift card, you can exchange it for cash on websites like GiftCardGranny.com, CardCash.com, or Cardpool.com.
667. Turn it into something else with some help from your creative side.
668. Try to return it for store credit.
669. Use it to barter for other things on websites like Craigslist.org or Kijiji.ca.
670. If all else fails, throw it out. Don't let it turn into clutter.

Index

Improve Your Life—
One Hack at a Time!

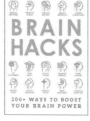